INSPIRED

By Raspy

CONTENT

PREFACE

Language shapes your thoughts. For instance. In some languages genders are attached to certain words, causing the reader to view not only the word, but also the origin differently. Than say someone from another region of the world. Think about reading right to left versus left to right.

Now think about having different words for different shades of colors instead of just Light and Dark, and how it shapes One's thoughts also. If you were given a point, and asked to measure distance from that point. Do you think your mind would work differently if your natural reaction were to measure vertically, instead of horizontally or vice versa.. hmmm.. Something to think about.

This book series spawned from Social Media. (Search Raspy Rawls) Overtime his writings became sort of like Modern Day Hieroglyphics to the Culture. The decoding of his words brings you into another world that teaches subconsciously and consciously how to overstand how Language shapes our thoughts, AND how much the English Language studs our ability to think.

12 topics were handpicked for Raspy to expound upon. The simplicity of his writings that cut so deep into the topic, without having to bore the reader with long nothingness. It's a signature of this Author's penmanship. His Insight along with Life Experiences should make this one hell of a read and experience.

"9. And the fourth was named Pênêmûe: he taught the children of men the bitter and the sweet; 10. And he pointed out to them every secret of their wisdom. 11. He taught man to understand writing with ink and paper. 12. Therefore numerous have been those who have gone astray from every period of the world, even to this day. 13. For men were not born for this, thus with pen and with ink to give confirm their faith with pen and ink;" (Cepher 68. 9-13)

INTRODUCTION

In order for you to fully grasp anything beyond this page, please read the following 3 Definitions 7x before proceeding..

Full Definition of read: read play \ˈred\ reading play \ˈrē-diŋ\

transitive verb

1a (1) : to receive or take in the sense of (as letters or symbols) especially by sight or touch (2) : to study the movements of (as lips) with mental formulation of the communication expressed (3) : to utter aloud the printed or written words of <read them a story> b : to learn from what one has seen or found in writing or printing.

http://www.merriam-webster.com

Full Definition of Comprehension

noun

1a : the act or action of grasping with the intellect : understanding b : knowledge gained by comprehending c: the capacity for understanding fully <mysteries that are beyond our comprehension>

2a : the act or process of comprising b : the faculty or capability of including : comprehensiveness

http://www.merriam-webster.com

CONTEXT CLUE

noun

a method by which the meanings of unknown words may be obtained by examining the parts of a sentence surrounding the word fordefinition/explanation clues,restatement/synonym clues, contrast/antonymclues, and inference/general context clues.

http://www.Dictionary.com

MEDIA VS SOCIAL MEDIA

Whoever controls the images controls the mind.. The mind is THEE MOST POWERFUL THANG ON EARTH YERME.. Thought is God.. Without Thought NOTHING gets done.. How pure or perverted are your thoughts.. Be honest witcha self yerme.. They say Art Imitates Life.. Well there's this patent (US 6506148) you should look into.. In jail you fuk around and get killed behind the TV. The World's biggest leisure is watching TV.

Your subconscious don't know reality from TV.. That's why we produce emotions watching TV. And on TV you watch wat.. A PROGRAM.. A program to program who and program who to dew wat eggzactly.. Hmmmm.. So who programmed the program.. Who pays that programmer.. Wait.. All that's controlled by 6 companies.. Soooo.. *scratches head*.. Yes.. It's true.. We've been programmed to sleep..

Reality in most people's minds are not one of their own creation..
Our entire life is decided for us and our poe parents have no fukn
clue wat they're dewin when they sign us off after birth.. Debt slaves
to the Crown.. Soul slaves to Rome The Vatican The Fake Jews and
da devil.. All the same lineage.. They've taken over the minds of the
Chosen Children.. Then the Internet came..

And Social Media happened.. And people were able to share information they have from Life Experiences or from reading other thangs than from 6 controlled sources.. We don't use Social Media like we should.. So Eye wrote a book (The Revolutionary Guide to Social Media). Not only will Eye teach you how to use Social Media..

Eye will also give examples of wat has and hasn't werked the past 6 years for me in my quest to Deprogram then Reprogram Our Minds.. That's why as of Oct. 1, 2016 OimmaBombYa turned the USA's Internet over Internationally.. Social Media is a problem for them.. And everyone cept The People of the USA know this.. Like the world is awaiting for us over hea to wake up..

They all know their leaders are corrupted thru the illusion of white supremacy.. We're the only ones still asleep to it collectively.. And until Social Media no one outside of the USA overstood why really.. Now they can see how mind fukd in education and robbed of our identity we are.. Now with Trump in office, the veil is being lifted even moor yerme.. And Eye'm loving it lol..

RELIGION

Ancient Ways of Living Perverted by Man to fit his evilness.. So if you go back and study the History of Ancient Cultures and the way they ACTUALLY lived, you'll start to recognize how fukd up Religion really is lol.. Religion is wat MAN created NOT The Most High..

P.S. The Most High doesn't have a Religion..

BIBLE

The Bible is just the latest version of Ancient Text from our Ancestors..The problem is once ppl find out the Europeans tampered with the text they throw it away.. Instead of going find the corrections.. We are conditioned to look at the Bible as a Religious Book thru a Eurocentric POV.. When it's actually a History Book from some Africans.. Yes Africans.. Africa is a Continent.. Not a Country or Nation..

Isreal and Iraq, Syria, so called Middle East.. Allat is North East Africa.. There is No such thang as the Middle East.. The Man-made Suez Canal is what is used to condition ppl to believe the lie.. History Book that contains something our communities need so badly.. Morals.. Laws.. Principles.. Discipline.. Wisdom.. Knowledge.. Science.. Math.. Anatomy.. Etc.. And the further back into the text you go.. The moor you start to unlock a lot of life's secrets..

Studying Hebrew was beneficial to unlocking my language code.. Eye view languages different now.. Knowing letters have characteristics and numerical value and are read right to left.. LEARN HOW TO READ THE BIBLE BEFORE YOU ATTEMPT TO BELIEVE THE BIBLE.. Don't just go out thea believing anything.. Our Ancestors.. A large amount of them.. Used this way of life to succeed..

And as Eye look around.. We don't actually read the Bible.. We just talk Bible.. Cause if you actually did we'd see wats going on in the church is not wat the Bible says.. But the Bible not telling you nothing you ain't heard before.. Or don't naturally feel as a human.. Same thing with our Ancestors.. This shyt was Universal Knowledge.. Everybody knew the Laws of the Land.. The Most High don't change.. We just disobedient..

Harriet Tubman Marcus Garvey Nat Turner all had the Sword as their foundation.. That's wat we need to be tryna evoke in our sleep headed ass family members.. It's not gonna be easy cause they feel if they look left or right their world crashes forever.. When in actuality you come to life.. Yano how tight a hold the Pope has on the South when it comes to the Bible..

Eye even have Mama Raspy starting to dew moor research.. Reading other material outside the Bible.. This Research Group will put a lot of thangs in proper context from our POV.. Your Eyes will open up to a new world.. Ever wonder how Eye have so much insight on shyt.. The Bible lol.. Eye tell this to my friends all the time.. And Eye'ma leave this with you..

The overstanding you're missing in life.. Comes from not knowing how to read the Bible AND the Ancient Text it all comes from.. It changed my life.. AND STILL has my life getting better and better by the day.. #JordanShrug

P.S. Go Back to Sumer Ur Mesopotamia.. AND the AMERICAS.. We're leaving too many pieces untouched since Egypt is always highlighted.. #ThinkAboutIt

MOTHER OF CIVILIZATION/WOMBMAN

The Most Disrespected Being on the Planet is The Mother of Civilization.. And it's our Fault.. Men/Kangs/Brothers.. Yes Us.. If it wasn't bad enuff she was Raped during slavery.. Torn away from her cheerun.. Impregnated by massa.. And na we've turned all our anger toward our women.. Smh.. Eye'm ashamed personally.. Eye think we need to bring "Shame" back.. We have lost all our Manners and Morals..

Our Queens are so objectified that they have been conditioned to Lead with their bodies.. And are so confused they get mad cause when we Lead off with wat she puts into the spotlight.. It's a never ending cycle at this rate.. Eye'ma firm believer that if Our Queens had their standards elevated.. Then Our Kangs would have to elevate theirs.. Cause you not gonna get no pussy from a Queen while you're in peasant status.. That Knowledge of Self is not having that shyt lol..

So Eye been on a mission to elevate you Queens.. See Eye remember running the streets.. And although my first marriage didn't last.. Eye, Me, Personally locked in moor and focused moor having a Queen on my side.. She's the Ying to our Yang.. We can never find Balance Harmony nor Peace if we don't find it WITH OUR QUEENS.. It's just not happening yerme..

So if you think you gonna WIN IN LIFE.. You better get a SiStar..

A Real SiStar.. Speshlee us American Kangs.. No other woman can

connect with you and your struggle in America the way she can..

Be gentle with them.. Yet stay firm.. If you build Her up on Love &

Truth.. She'll bring you places you couldn't get into yourself yerme..

In the Torah it says Sin entered the world thru MAN, NOT WOMAN.. It was man that wasn't gentle yet firm with her to take a stand.. The Feminist Movement.. The Famous Pic of Gloria Steinem and Michele Wallace for the Feminist Movement.. Pretty sho you seen the pic.. Well Gloria was a CIA agent who used Michele as the face of "We Hate Black Men", for the gumment..

This to me was the last time we didn't protect Our Queens.. No Eye'm lion.. This new Gay shyt.. Eye watched women turn gay for a paycheck.. Smh.. With all that said.. We need to werk on our Mental Health.. Individually Collectively and Community wise.. We gotta elevate Our Queens.. They carry Nations.. They carry US.. So this wat we gon dew..

Eye'ma start Counseling Our Queens.. Strengthening their intellect..

And if you,my Kang Brother, want my Queen SiStar.. You gonna

have requirements to reach.. We already know the gumment took the

Men out the house to take their place and disrupt The Most High's

Family Structure.. Which means we must use this to our advantage..

We must encourage Our Queens to learn all the Systems they give her access to.. And bring that data back to the table.. We see how they have changed the playing field.. We gon audible or run the ball with a blitz coming..

And Eye know some of yall saying wat you got to say directly to the women.. NOTHING.. Us men didn't build yall no system for yall to blossom in.. Eye need us Men to get back into the way of putting our Community & Family First.. Before Anything.. So all the women who are reading this.. Make sho erry man in your life reads this.. Thanks.. Love You Queen.. KANG ♛

P.S. Queens follow The Most High.. If he wants really wants you he'll have no problem going beyond the call..

NATIONALITY

The status of belonging to a particular Nation.. Legally.. African American is NOT a Nationality.. There's no African American Government Flag Constitution nothing.. We ain't shyt but property under this African American Status.. That's how come police can murder us and get away with it.. That's how come thea is no law saying you have to pay taxes.. Yet you still pay them..

And no you don't have to be a Moor to Stand on the Law.. BUT YOU.. And nobody else but YOU.. Can Stand on the Law for YOU at all times.. Nobody gon be around yo Lil uglass all the time.. Therefore YOU need to be sharp on your game yerme.. And that's what Nationality does.. It forces you to have to study Law so that you don't sign verbal or written contracts without first knowing WTF they're talmbot..

YOUR SIGNATURE/WERD IS THE MOST IMPORTANT THANG IN THIS ILLUSION OF WHITE SUPREMACY.. AS IN LIFE ALSO.. Yano.. Werd is BOND B lol.. Me personally.. Eye want Nationality for a lot of reasons.. Eye want my community to be able to dew business with our Brother and Sister Nations without asking permission from kkkrakkkas.. Everythang we dew is governed by some fukn kkkrakkkas..We want Reparations.. Go to kkkrakkkas at UN.. Mannnnnn fuk allat..

How bout we become a fukn Nation.. Get with our Sibling Nations..

And hold ALLLLLLL THESE KKKRAKKKAS ACCOUNTABLE..

From them fake ass jews all the way down to the hillbilly rednecks

yerme.. Why we can't govern ourselves.. Why we can't police

ourselves.. Why we can't grow export cook and feed ourselves..

Why we can't build curriculums and teach ourselves.. Why we can't defend ourselves.. Why we can't vote on our own Leaders.. Why we can't establish Fortune 500 profitable businesses and employ our own.. WE CAN.. AND WE WILL..

THE SOLUTION.. HOW WE UNITE, ORGANIZE, AND NATIONALIZE.. https://www.amazon.com/Solution-Africans-America-Achieve-Justice-ebook/dp/B01LXEN0AM

AGRICULTURE

If every Truck Driver shut down for 2 weeks.. Wat would you eat after week one.. Like if nobody said nothing.. And the food slowly disappeared day by day without being restocked.. Wat would you dew.. How would your family eat.. How would yall survive??

If everythang you eat is poisonous cancer causing DNA altering genetically modified food.. And the Cancer Treatment was deadly, painful, depressingly ill to fatal, sometimes recovery but disfigurement may occur.. Or it may come back and you may beat it.. But you gotta take these pills that have side effects..That will cause you moor problems..

So here's some moor pills for those side problems.. Wait.. Don't forget the side of side effects from the pills that are taken for the side effects from the pills you took for the cancer from the food.. How would your lineage continue to survive??

If all animals went extinct.. That means no food from em.. No materials from em.. No fat from em.. Wat you gon eat?? Wat yall gon wear.. Louis Gucci Prada lmao.. How yall gon survive??

P.S. THE REVOLUTION HAS ALWAYS BEEN ABOUT LAND.. IF YOU DON'T CONTROL YOUR OWN FOOD SOURCE YOU'RE A SLAVE.. FOOD IS MEDICINE AND SO IS CANNABIS.. HEMP WILL REVOLUTIONIZE THE WORLD.. GO GREEN!!

COONS/SELLOUTS

A Coon is someone who intentionally and wilfully sides or sells out with oppressor for their own personal gain or protection.. SELLING OUT IS THE SAME AS SNITCHIN.. Stop selling out you lil bitty bitch you lol..Na there's a difference between SELLING OUT.. And being DRAWN

OUT.. Some of us are drawn out.. We're the smart ones.. Or the athletic ones.. Or the poetic ones..

Think about the financial gap between the Rich and Poor in everyone's community.. Ours have the largest gap.. The ones that make it are so far removed from those at the bottom til it's embarrassing honestly.. Sickening.. It really is a disease.. Something we must deal with.. It also happens in the "Movement/Non Profit" Sector.. Ferguson Eye had the front row seat.. They are vultures when it comes to making sho the influential ones get drawn out yerme..

Eye suggest that those that get drawn out our community or are already drawn, be assigned a "Conscious Advisor".. Or whatever fukn name we would agree on.. We could form an organization/ business around this idea.. Don't take much to develop this idea into a system.. America's Education System is an Intelligence Neutralizer.. Until Social Media.. We couldn't expect those drawn out to overstand the ills of society..

Yall know they let the jocks pass thru school without learning..
Easier draw out.. Duhhhh.. It's chess not checkers.. So we can't
sit and just let it continue.. Speshlee after Kaepernick and shyt..
The People are waking up.. And it's up to those who have already
crossed that path to help guide others.. Anyone who has an influence
over our community should be advised by someone conscious to the
times we're living in..

Now back to you Coon sellout trick bitches.. You bitches are the worst cause history shows you wat happens to yo lil dumbass too.. And you still make that decision.. They killed Malcom and Martin.. Violent or Non Violent.. And your status gives you a view most don't get so we know you see the shyt.. Death to you traitors!!

VOTING

Gonna make this short and sweet yerme.. We get hung up on this too much.. Everyone screams how can this system fail you when it wasn't designed to serve you..Well if that is correct.. How can you expect your vote to EVER create the change that's needed in a system that was designed to fail you.. It will never happen..

You don't control the Electoral College who chooses the president. Although 24 states have laws stating they must select who majority of the people of that state votes for.. But who TF believes these kkkrakkkas are trustworthy after studying history..

Now voting locally does have a moor direct effect on you and your family.. But it's STILL the same system from the top.. Same system that wasn't designed to see you succeed.. Create your own system.. Start werkin on one in your mind and bring it into reality.. And be fukn realistic.. Creating non practical solutions are useless..

P.S. VOTE WITH YOUR POCKET.. BUY BLACK BUT SELL TO ERRYBODY.. GROW SOME SHYT..YOU WILL NOT VOTE AWAY YOUR OPPRESSOR, USING YOUR OPPRESSOR'S SYSTEM..

PRESIDENT OIMMABOMBYA

Ion even know if OimmaBombYa is even an actual person anymoor.. Is he chipped.. Is he cloned.. Like yo WTF.. Ion really be talmbot it too much cause he's done being the face of oppression in the world. Wait, Trump Won.. Lemme not speak too to fast lmao.. Might Martial Law Suspend the Constitution 3rd Term our asses lol.. Can't lie.. He did his job tho..

The job of luring yo black uglass back to sleep after ignorant ass C grade having ass pussy ass lil Bush controlled demolition of the towers and flooded my state and put those Acts they were already committing in the dark into law.. It's chess not checkers.. OimmaBombYa knew eggzactly wat was at risk..

You don't getta be President and not know WTF is going on.. And you ppl who think he's clueless and just tryna help but Congress is stopping him.. Funny how nobody stopped him, not even his beautiful wife and daughters, nor himself.. From signing a fukn Blue Lives Matter fukn Bill.. Also the NDAA.. When you're protecting the Slave Catchers and expanding Slavery, how else am Eye sposta feel.. #FOMF

We put our faith in person who's job was to be a the PERFECT HOUSE NIGGER..

Seriously think about it.. He went became The Face of Massa's House.. After massa made us build it for him and his family.. Eye didn't say he over thru massa and took massa house.. Eye said he became THE FACE OF MASSA'S HOUSE.. And wat has massa been known to be towards folk who look like me throughout history.. RIIIIIGHT!! Next...

BLACK LIVES MATTER

Black Lives Mattered before the Organization was ever thought of. If Black Lives didn't matter, we wouldn't continue to be kidnapped and held captives in those jails and penitentiaries for cheap labor. They Mattered when the US Government Assassinated Martin, Malcolm, Nat Turner, Gabriel Prosser, gave Ali the shakes, raised Assata bounty to 2 million dollars, stole Henrietta Lacks cells after her death to create technology to extend their lives and make billions before anyone even knew anything, and melanin by gram is higher than gold.

And that's just in America.. So yeah, Black Lives ALWAYS Mattered. And NO, we don't need an organization funded by our known enemies that has proven to infiltrate movements and cause division. Give you an example.. Personal Experience of mine, and to me yerme, it's was the biggest stage of all so far to date.. FERGUSON.. THE WHOLE ENTIRE WORLD WAS WATCHING FERGUSON.

But all yall really saw was the protest and interviews and shyt.. Yall didn't getta witness the 10s of thousands of dollar meetings that went on. Some meetings maybe for 2-3 days.. Those Big Billionaires fly in those ACTORvist and the passive aggressive games start taking place. Gender Pronouns and bullshyt like that..

Like you don't know in your attire if you're a man or woman let alone your sexual preference and hair style. Yet you expect a Brother off the block to automatically call you a HE, when you're born a SHE, and we just got him to finally start calling a few women Queens. Like Mental Health notta problem in our community..

So the Brothers off the block get pushed out and made to feel uncomfortable.. And the Sister off the Block gets turned out.. Yeah, that part.. But yall don't hear me tho yerme.. Just check the organization's website.. Shrugs..

P.S. Ferguson was the longest stance we've had in our community since Martin & Malcolm and The Civil Rights Movement.. And BLM helped break that up.. Every other Uprising since has been quickly silenced.. And who's always at the forefront.. Think About That..

LONG LIVE MY BROTHER AND COMRADE KANG DARREN SEALS!!

KKKRAKKKA EUROPEANS

Eye believe they are of another species. Not the same as the Original HueMan species of the planet. History shows them to be very destructive savage animalistic war mongering destroyers Collectively. Also willfully ignorant, must be beas.. naaa.. Cause animals are intelligent. They're cancerous. When something is as cancerous as this, what is the normal protocol, and why aren't we using it. Feelings aside. If everyone cared so much about the planet and it's survival, why aren't they addressing the problem.

Even other Europeans, in USA and abroad. Speshlee USA. Yall dew allat fukn bragging bout, "That's because whites make up majority". Why don't yall make up majority of yall minds and find yall Origin and and stop yall brothers who yall swear is only a few bad apples. Can't brag about one, and not dew anything about the other.

Oh, and another thang. Just because Eye believe they're evil, doesn't mean Eye go around being ugly to them. Ion go around being ugly to anybody. Not in my nature. We Lead they Follow.. #LevelUp Dew Eye think Europeans are the devil. Eye'm just saying, Eye ain't never seen the two in the same room together yerme lol..

P.S. Be God Body

POLICE AKA SLAVE PATROL

Louisiana is the world's prison capital. FACT!! Louisiana is one of the worst States in Education in the U.S. FACT!! The 13th Amendment allows for Slavery to take place in the account that a crime was committed, and you are found guilty. FACT!! Reread the opening line up top again for me please.. Let it sink in. Incarceration is BIG BUSINESS. Free labor is the reason Lincoln went to war.

The Southern States, with the help of Free Slave Labor, would eventually take over the North economically had Chattel Slavery continued. After Lincoln's Assassination, the South Elected ex-Confederate Leaders in positions of power. Knowing they had recently went to war over the abolishment of slavery, why would one believe their actions would change. Here to tell you they didn't. Black Codes, which mirrored those of colonial time, were implemented to continue to oppress the now freed American Aboriginal and the Imported African Slave.

The Vagrancy Law was used to force the Freedmen to sign Labor Contracts as Black "Servants" for White "Masters". Being that you were arrested for not having a job, which in return meant you would have to work a job regardless. Just with no pay this time. You could overstand why some Freedmen would sign the Labor Contracts.

}

Fast forward to the murdering of Alton Sterling. The Black Codes were enforced by the Slave Patrol. Virginia, North Carolina, South Carolina were first in creating slave patrol units. The officers in these units were called patrollers, which etymologically comes from the French word pattroulier. Thus we get the modern term Pat-rol/Patrol officers, in later years, Patrol officers became general police officers for all communities.

The vibration from which this arm of the system was founded on has continued to live and thrive openly and aggressively. So aggressively two patrol officers were allowed to tackle a father of 5, restrict movement of both hands, yell gun, publicly execute him on camera, and still go home to their families with pay. Behavior which has always been openly present in the South, but with the creation of camera phones and Social Media, the world now sees this behavior is present EVERYWHERE!!

Everyone should be outraged that behavior has gone on this long, at this rate. But they're not, and that speaks to an even bigger problem. A systematic one. One that conditions society to treat a group of people less than humane, and conditions the rest to believe they deserve it. Let's be honest. NO ONE DESERVES THIS!! A sure sign of measurement would be to ask those groups would they switch places with the other. Their responses might leave you frozen for a moment.

The patrol officers should be disarmed and completely stopped based off it's foundation. That would require the admittance of the injust Judicial System, by the ones who created and maintain it. You must be able to find the root of our problems, unbiasedly, and create solutions for those problems. Americans who are melanin dominant are 2.5 times more likely to be shot and killed by the patrol officers than their counterparts. They are convicted more, and face stiffer sentencing also.

The formation of their own government which would include their own enforcers of their laws, similar to the Natives, should be a place of orientation. If we saw police officers as the Slave Patrolman they are, rather than Law Enforcement.. Then maybe we'd remember who they REALLY are..

AUTHOR

Raspy Rawls is an International Community Organizer, Social Media Guru, Social Justice Activist, Hip Hop Artist, Counselor, Mentor, and Educator. Raspy is the Chief Executive Officer and Founder of the Raspy Rawls Brand. Co Founder of the Up Community Brand. A & R at the Blazin Streetz Brand. All three serve as different platforms to relay a positive message to The People.

From High School Star Athlete to two-time college dropout to losing his 100 Ton Captain's License to a Drug Charge and jail time, it's safe to say. Raspy has really used his life experiences as crutches to hold him up, rather than hold him back. It shows in the way he leverages those Life Experiences to light a path for the Most Known to Unknowns of the world.

Made in the USA
Columbia, SC
20 October 2020